HAPPY
60
AFTER

Hacking Life Habits and Planning Your Best Life At The End

Written by:

Napoleon Forte

CONTENTS

INTRODUCTION

This past summer was a milestone for me, as I reached the respectable age of 60. I'm still grappling with this transition into my seventh decade of life. Turning 60 feels somehow weightier than turning 59 just a year ago. They say age is just a number, but this particular number gives me pause.

I find myself doing some soul-searching about this new phase of life I'm entering.

What does it mean to be 60?

Of course, it's different for everyone, but for me, there's a certain sense of taking stock at this point. I'm looking back over the arc of my life so far, while also thinking ahead to the years yet to come.

There are new aches and pains, yes, reminders of the passage of time. But there is also new wisdom borne of experience, and a desire to simplify and focus on what matters most. I know some of you can relate to being at this crossing between midlife and later years. Perhaps you have your complicated feelings about leaving your 50s behind. While all of our stories are unique, I think there is a universality in facing the milestones that urge us to reflect. This is just my personal experience, but I'm sure many can understand the self-examination that significant birthdays like 60 can inspire.

In many ways, entering a new decade feels liberating — I strive to care less about the small stuff and superficial matters. Yet, it also brings its sense of mortality into sharper focus. I realize I likely now have less road ahead of me than what lies behind me in the rear-view mirror. That reality lends itself to an urgency to make the most of every passing second.

I want to nurture the relationships that matter most. I want to offer my knowledge and experience to help lift others. I want to keep learning, growing, and exploring this complex world we inhabit. There are still goals to pursue and contributions to make. In other words, I don't feel done yet! Sixty is not the end of the road for me.

Yes, parts of my body remind me I'm not as spry as I used to be. But my spirit and mind feel young, perhaps younger now than in my actual youth. I have a sense of clarity and purpose that only comes with age and experience. I know myself better, and I accept myself more fully. And I think that self-awareness and authenticity lend themselves to deeper connections, to seeing the beauty all around us.

C. JOYBEL says, "We must not fear change".

You may feel very secure in the pond you are in, but if you never leave it, you will never be exposed to the idea that there is such a thing as an ocean or a sea.

Change can be scary - believe me, I understand. When life feels stable and predictable, we tend to cling to what's familiar. It's human nature. I should know, because I've often resisted change myself, preferring the comfort of my little "pond" to the vast unknown "ocean" of new possibilities.

Yet I've learned that staying too confined within our small worlds holds us back from growth and discovery. We need to take risks and venture forth, even when change feels uncertain or intimidating. In my experience, those who resist change remain limited in their perspectives and unable to envision broader horizons.

As one who has gradually stepped out of my comfort zone over the years, I assure you - the ocean is waiting for you too. And though its tides may be tumultuous at times, floating in those uncharted waters has brought me wonders I never could have imagined. When we open our minds, expand beyond the familiar, and face our fears - that's when life surprises us with its extraordinary beauty.

So come, friend, let's be bold - dip your toes in, wade out, sail forth! Great joy awaits us in the vast seas of possibility that live within and around us. The view from here is breathtaking. And I'll be right here sailing beside you along the way.

So in many ways, 60 feels like a beginning, not an ending. If I take care of myself, who knows how many vibrant years lie ahead? I choose to face this decade with an open heart, fully present for whatever this part of the journey has in store. I hope anyone facing a significant milestone birthday can relate to and embrace both the poignancy and promise of their maturing years. The adventure continues...shall we see where it leads?

CHAPTER ONE
Take me Back to where it Began

Why not start the holiday season with that loved conventional - Planes, Trains and Automobiles? Ever since Jeanie and I first noticed it again in 1987, we have made it our little culture to watch this comedy gem every 12 months on Tuesdays. We had been simply 25 years antique newlyweds, excited to start our traditions together.

I nevertheless take into account how a whole lot we laughed at Steve Martin's epic and hilariously disastrous adventure to make it home for the holiday. All the travel mishaps he encounters while reluctantly teamed up with the lovely motor-mouth performed by the late John Candy. It changed into amusing watching the mismatched pair slowly bond amidst the chaos of their misfortunes.

All those years later, now in our 60s, Planes, Trains and Automobiles have become nostalgic for Jeanie and me. We recognize the jokes by coronary heart, of course, but it brings us lower back to the early days of our marriage every time we watch it. We cuddle up with popcorn similar to what we did in our little first condominium, awaiting the vacation season collectively.

It's our quirky manner of easing into Thanksgiving coaching amidst all of the bustle and busyness this time of 12 months brings. No, remember what else goes on, we carve out this unique date night to experience this traditional comedy. The story of a not-like friendship shaped by a turbulent adventure reminds us to lean on every other, whilst times get hard or unpredictable. It allows us to have a good time and gratitude for having a loving accomplice to proportion life's many adventures with.

So because the leaves turn and fall settles in, we excitedly are counted right down to our cherished film night kickoff. Let the comfort food, excursion cheer and belly laughs start! Does anyone else have a favourite movie they watch every year to usher inside the most wonderful time of the year?

It's tough to accept as true with Steve Martin becoming already 42 while Planes, Trains & Automobiles debuted back in '87. He plays Neil Page so convincingly - the instantly-laced marketing guy desperately scrambling to get home to his photo-best suburban circle of relatives in time for Thanksgiving dinner. I recall referring to Neil's mounting anxiety and frustration as disaster after disaster derailed his journey plans.

Neil's urgency to make it home was so palpable - with an affected person's wife and three babies eagerly awaiting his arrival for the vacation festivities. Meanwhile, I pictured his tidy brick residence all aglow, the desk set flawlessly, Norman Rockwell-esque turkey waiting to be carved. Neil's cautiously orchestrated life coming unglued set the degree for huge laughs...And a surprisingly huge coronary heart.

Of course, the overdue John Candy stole many scenes as Neil's undesirable journey associate - the affable, awkward, nonstop chatterbox, Del Griffith. Turns out he's a wanderlust bathe curtain ring salesman lacking any real roots or domestic to talk of. Del simply latches onto Neil's determined assignment to make it to Chicago in time for turkey dinner.

I received Smash whatever in case you haven't had the pride of seeing this 80s comedy gem yet. Let's just say Neil arrives at his image-perfect suburban home a full day overdue for Thanksgiving dinner - dishevelled, exhausted with unlikely new buddy Del in tow. The look on his wife's face seeing this unusual couple on her doorstep after weathering a travel nightmare neither ought to be planned for.

That ultimate poignant scene makes you consider how often existence sends us detours and probabilities to connect in sudden approaches. The movie reminds us now not to sweat the small stuff and lean into life's imperfections - no vacation desk or tour plan is ever quite as polished as we envision. But connection and information may be discovered in not going places if we preserve an open coronary heart.

Losing the ones we love from the elder generation over the years leaves a profound void. I nonetheless feel my mum and dad's absence acutely all through the vacations and milestone moments they ought to be here to percentage. Knowing Jeanie feels that ache too over her dad's passing nonetheless brings me sorrow.

And, Jeanie's 90-year-antique mom has grown to be a testament to lifestyles's patience and resilience. Well into her 10th decade yet still so mentally sharp, playful and wise - she amazes me daily. She includes the flames of reminiscence for generations past so fantastically for all people.

I think that poignant function evolves to the elder's left status - to be the heartbeat bridging the day before this and the day after today. I aspire to grow in that grace the manner Jeanie's mother fashions so certainly in her vulnerable age.

Perhaps the empty areas left behind make the hand we will nonetheless maintain rather more precious. Missing one's beloved ghosts is the rate of ardour and attachment. But gratitude grows too for every smile, hug and handclasp with those still taking walks on this adventure with us.

Maybe that was the last message for Neil ultimately - coming to peer Del now not as a nuisance but as a fellow sojourner, on my own but worthy of connection and care. Life whittles our numbers as years pass, however, new possibilities to link arms and hearts continue to be all around.

My challenge now could be to carry the misplaced ones inside while embracing every soul - younger, elder or fellow traveller - nonetheless blessing me with their light. The generations are bound via love, on this international or the next.

When you lose a discern young, their passing feels premature, a life unfinished. Standing beside my father's grave at 58, I imagined how jarring and incomprehensible this give-up could feel to my boyhood self. Childhood seems countless when you're in it - how ought to any kid fathom existence's fleeting nature or the sorrow of burying 1/2 your family years later?

Yet right here I stand these days, six hundred miles from domestic, searching out over the hillside cemetery in old-fashioned Front Royal protecting the earthly remains of my sister, dad and mom. Half of my adolescent own family, all long passed before their time. I go to after I can, tending their headstones, the icy wind biting at my ageing cheeks as I ponder the atypical brevity of all of it.

Attending a scholars' convention currently, I was struck with the aid of a brand new sensation - I had emerged as one of the elder statesmen in my subject. I realized my era now filled most keynote speeches and primary periods, at the same time as huge-eyed college students and early profession oldsters peppered the audiences. When did I become the mentor as opposed to the mentee?

Rather than depressing, this dawning becomes oddly hopeful, hinting at the continuity amid existence's churning cycles. My mentors are buried here beneath the Virginia soil, but their thoughts, passions and guidance live on through my paintings. In turn, I now get to pay that getting to know forward through the subsequent technology simply starting off to leave their mark.

The young parents listening in rapt attention rekindled my sense of surprise and discovery even all these years later. Their eager minds maintain plasticity and promise my ossifying views may also increasingly lack. Together our speak holds the energy of alchemy - taking the know-how of beyond generations to gas breakthroughs neither I nor they might attain alone.

This abnormal kinship of ages soothing my spirit amidst the long goodbyes, I realise the professors resting right here might be proud. Their light incorporates through me and limitless others whose sights they helped expand. And now I stand equipped to lend my shoulder to clean minds quickly to tackle what we could not complete. The endless cycle keeps lifestyles sincerely unfinished.

Attending this 12-month conference, I couldn't help but word the absence of such a lot of mentors and seminal thinkers who fashioned me. The halls felt empty without their understanding and familiar faces. Of direction, COVID in all likelihood saved some of the elder statesmen away, prioritizing precautions. But the reality is, that so many pioneers in my field have passed in only the previous few years.

My dear professor Ron Sider left us in advance this year. I audibly gasped after I heard the news. I pictured Ron's kind smile, his ardour for justice, and the way his publications lit a heart in me to technique theology extra courageously. Even months later, tears sting my eyes knowing I can't shoot him an update on my budding research or how his teaching took root in me.

The stark fact at 60 is maximum who moulded my wondering over time now are living in the cemetery, not the lecture corridor. Their memorial career programs are stacked in my office - mentors, guiding lighting fixtures, beloved teachers now ghostly memories but ever-present influences. I assume as their scholar, part of my role now could be channelling their ethos, building on their rhetorical shoulders.

But oh how I omit them! That twinkle in Ron's eye when he endorsed loudly for society's outcasts. The manner of Dr. Ryan's poetry lecturing made theology sing. Dr. Smith's rapier wit paired with such gentleness. They prepared me to carry torches now growing heavy in my weary grip.

My young friends look on quizzically as I choke up discussing those greats now long gone. They can not hold close the enormity of this sea change - to be orphaned from the scholarly lineage that birthed your reason and direction. My world has been upended, and with so many guides now etched in stone, I mourn the remaining vestiges of my wide-eyed, naive teens.

And yet...Here I stand, populated by using their very ideas and ethics. I concentrate more closely while younger scholars proportion. I am seeking out their articles first, eager for fresh insights from fertile minds. I aspire to inspire their talents now too, to hold my mentors' values thriving. The flower might also wilt however its nectar and seeds propel the subsequent garden. This painting usually maintains.

Becoming the patriarch of my circle of relatives lineage at simply 60 years vintage feels almost premature, although I do cherish the role. Losing each dad and mom this beyond decade caused my siblings and me to suddenly elderly into the elder statesmen of our extended family.

My relatives jokingly dub me "Gushee Senior" these days in our huge brood's institution texts and at rowdy own family reunions. And I ought to admit, being the sage vintage soul on the kids' desk does warm my coronary heart, at the same time as I nevertheless feel quite spry and young at coronary heart myself!

We these days amassed four living generations around the Thanksgiving desk – from Jeanie's stylish ninety-yr-antique mother down to our bubbly 4-yr-vintage grandbaby. A new grandkid due in January will further enlarge our bustling family tree.

As I gazed lovingly at all the long-time guffawing collectively, I marvelled at the breadth of continuity throughout our circle of relatives' timeline. Jeanie's mom nevertheless tells shiny tales of her grandparents born around 1900. And our grandbabies frolicking together may nicely stay till 2100 and beyond.

Nearly 170 years of circle of relatives reminiscences bridged before my eyes! What a splendid privilege to anchor the central bankruptcy of that tale as a proud patriarch. The responsibility to proportion and guard all we've learned lived and overcome feels without delay heavy and holy.

Of direction, the cycle of lifestyles insists new shoots have to update old boom in due time. But for now, I drink up this wealthy intermingling of views at our crowded dinner desk. One day the younger ones will reminisce about those moments with their families, perhaps calling my name fondly after they need strength or idea.

But nowadays, amid peals of laughter, I deliver thanks for the tapestry of overlapping lives naming me Gushee Senior. May we keep grafting our numerous branches collectively through many generations yet to come back in this circle of relatives' tree?

Turning 60 brings with it a positive wistful thinking beforehand to all I will miss seeing of my loved grandkids' lives unfolding. When little Mia catapults into my lap for spontaneous hugs, or Jacob begs for just one greater bedtime story, part of me mourns knowing I will most effectively percentage fleeting snippets of their trips.

Of course, while you're in the busy thick of midlife raising your young group, you are taking without any consideration that you'll usually be their depended-on anchor. Only later does the temporariness of lifestyles sink in. To realise I'll possibly only know Mia and Jacob as small kids - no longer the finished artists or marketers they will in the future turn out to be - fills me with sober nostalgia.

My getting older reflection inside the mirror predicts the relentless march of years I have left with them.

Such finite, valuable time! When did my hair and stamina start greying at the temples? Wasn't I bouncing my babes on my knee just the day before today before this aching arthritic knee?

No one warns you as a determine how unexpectedly those little palms you hold close will outgrow your very own. Yet here I stand on the point of Grandpa-hood at 60, lamenting all the dance recitals, graduations and wedding ceremony days I haven't witnessed in my grandkids' personal lives. Even the profound privilege of guiding them through adolescent developing pains won't be mine to proportion.

Still, I dangle to my position as their pioneering patriarch - supplying all I can at the same time as energy and time allow. Maybe I can equip them with sufficient love, laughter and life lessons now to ultimately lengthy once I'm long gone. And if I'm certainly lucky, just perhaps I'll defy the chances and be there to cheer their victories many decades down the road!

For now, I plan to absorb each magical second and milestone I can proportion right here at my top. My babies will most effectively recognize Grandpa as a silver fox. But I pick to agree that all my soul's pourings into them these days will blossom and preserve their flourishing lengthy once I rest.

And so the cycle spins on, infinite revolutions of life and loss. With my recent 60th milestone, I have stuck poignantly among generations beyond and those yet to spread.

I stand solemn as mentors' names now mark bloodless marble inside the cemetery, whilst their hearts and wisdom kindle nevertheless within me. The best homage is within the mild I now bypass to their keen protégés in outstretched fingers. My legacy shall be buffered against the bitter wind.

Behind me, a lineage 168 years inside the making still stretches robust. And by grace's hand, my grandbabies may additionally bring our family torch for over a century extra. At therapy's desk, we journey on.

Today at least, four generations improve a glass amid proud hugs and laughter that warms our hearts. I dangle at this fleeting intersection, flooding their cup to overflowing. May it quench longing long when I'm the ghost they toast.

For now, sweet infant voices name "Papa!" with abandon as we roast marshmallows using the crackling fire. Their tiny palms hold close to mine completely trusting our anchor will hold. Bathed in a golden glow, for this gilded moment now, it truly will.

CHAPTER TWO
Life – Passing the Torch

At 60 years old, I locate myself in an unusual role as a university professor - nonetheless active and enthusiastic about teaching, but acutely aware my time left in the classroom is limited. Academia is extra forgiving of growing old than most fields, valuing knowledge and experience. But even so, the sands in my professional hourglass are visibly dwindling.

With each clean crop of students, I'm starkly reminded of my mortality. Young scholars' vivid eyes shone again at me, eager for understanding and expertise to chart their paths in advance. Meanwhile, my mirrored image peering lower back seems weathered - while did this grey creep into my beard?

I laugh wondering how completely ancient 60 regarded from the alternative facet of the lectern years ago. Funny how time blurs once you're inhabiting a later lifestyle degree yourself. I nonetheless feel like that awestruck grad scholar in many approaches. Yet the students respectfully calling me "Doctor" reveals a conversion of guards well underway.

My route roster repeating on a 3-12 months cycle now feels all at once poignant. Just some extra probabilities continue to be to teach some of those loved classes I've honed over a long time. The finite nature makes every seminar session experience surprisingly precious, an unrepeatable opportunity for collected minds to interact, assign assumptions, and interconnect.

At times wistfulness sweeps over me knowing those may be my remaining years maintaining this exhilarating intellectual space. Yet channeling my mentor's spirit, I propose to ignite restless curiosity in students who will soon inherit the baton. To feed the ones sparks of their synapses, trusting they will convey the light ahead whilst my energy expires.

For now, as a minimum, ours is a lively dialogue between generations buying and selling equipment to demolish boundaries. We cobble awareness of each ancient and new. Together we shine more luminous than any unmarried flame should sustain. This sacred cycle persists, as timeless as it is fleeting.

As a public highbrow, I built my profession on probing novels, media statements and Twitter debates at the troubles of the day. But at 60, with most of my prolificacy behind me, I was prepared to allow the following generation's voices to take the mic. I've made my peace that the lion's proportion of my novels and critiques now reside inside the beyond.

It's odd to look at brilliant lecturers 15 years my junior now controlling the discourse and narratives I used to shape. But the relief of chickening out from Noise to nurture relationships and quieter pursuits is palpable. I depart the limitless debates and rivalries to people with greater fireplaces within the stomach.

With toughness in my circle of relatives, I can also yet have years beforehand. But brushing up in opposition to mortality at this age necessarily shifts the angle. Having lately misplaced peers and a sibling, I harbour no false hopes that the charging spectre of demise will pass me by. The stark fact is my flip in its crosshairs draws nigh.

I've long believed wrestling with the inevitability of death offers life's last spiritual assignment. But the cruellest injustice may be that by the time that reckoning arrives in advanced age, one's prime physical and intellectual colleges allowing that grappling have greatly dwindled. The very tools and acuity that had to manner and prepare for the cease are themselves finishing.

Watching my father bless every touring family member in his very last foggy days of hospice, I ached to figure out how his once bold IQ and perception had so eroded simply while he could've benefited most from those assets. It seems nearly a mocking cruelty of nature and time's unrelenting siege upon this mortal frame of ours.

And so, at the same time as my wits stay intact, I understand my paintings are to consciously face down demise earlier than it in addition encroaches. To proactively unpack this transition all of us must make, making peace with letting go of this worldly dance even as rhythm and mobility allow. Before the track fades, I have a few residing but to do. But I listen to the clock ticking toward my final bows.

CHAPTER THREE
What the End Looks Like

Given the inexorable march of time and going through my mortality, I now not suppose 60 feels premature to start consciously preparing for existence's very last transition. My fiery younger disdain for otherworldly orthodoxy that "over-spiritualized" death has softened. Now I better apprehend humans's deep need for help in grappling with the inevitable stop we all face.

In my early activism days, I joined a lot of friends hungering to create radical social exchange - to take place in God's Kingdom "on the planet as it is in heaven" through political transformation. But time has taught me the arena's entrenched brokenness will not be changing anytime quickly.

And even as scientific advances can be incrementally extending lifespans, loss of life stays the one absolute quandary no person escapes. At 60, the uneasy truth of my impermanence has replaced the cocksure invincibility of kids. Far from morbid, I've determined tremendous peace in sooner or later dealing with my demise with clean eyes.

The platitude "60 is the new forty" attempts to place an advantageous spin on matters, implying this level of life ought to experience equally colourful and efficient if we contend with ourselves. While I celebrate stepped forward health and hobby tiers allowing great durability, I additionally suppose it dangerous to keep off deeper wrestling with existential questions ageing tends to the floor.

I goal to stay completely whilst embracing my mortality - now not deny it through endless striving for fountain-of-children vitality. Mindful instruction for all aspects of my life's concluding chapter can unencumber that means-making and closure in a tradition captivated with hiding demise away.

I wish to method my final years with reverence and wonder at the sacred privilege of fully inhabiting every second I'm given. Making peace with endings opens space for deeper connections, for pouring love into this global knowing our time is precious. With grace, possibly I can guide others in their journeys grappling with life's ephemeral nature as well.

In the no longer-so-distant past, existence spread out like a predictable story. Back in 1970, the curtain on your operating days in all likelihood fell at round 64, giving you a leisurely six-and-a-1/2 years to bask in retirement before the grand finale. But similar to a plot twist in a nicely-worn novel, matters have changed dramatically. Modern medicine has ended up a wizard, waving its wand in opposition to infection and increasing our wholesome years some distance beyond everyone's wildest dreams. Smoking, after the ubiquitous villain, has lost its grip, and fitness focus has become a contemporary accent. As a result, the ones turning 60 in 2010 could confidently envision themselves not simply running the entire decade, but also taking part in a colourful lifestyle until a minimum of 78.7 years old. That's an additional 14 valuable years as compared to our opposite numbers from 1970 – sufficient time to jot down an entire new chapter, filled with adventures, passions, and perhaps even a 2d profession! So ditch the vintage retirement script and embody the exciting rewrite. Your 60s are just the beginning of a new act, full of possibilities waiting to be explored.

Transformational breakdown

- 1970: Retirement age – 64; Life expectancy – 70.8 years.
- 2010: Retirement age (flexible); Life expectancy – 78.7 years for 60-year-olds.

The key ingredients in this life-extending cocktail?

- *Medical Marvels:*

From gene-editing therapies to robotic surgeries, medicine is constantly pushing the boundaries of what's possible.

- *Smoking's Retreat:*

Thanks to public health campaigns and changing attitudes, cigarettes are losing their appeal, granting lungs (and overall health) a much-needed reprieve.

- *Wellness Revolution:*

Fitness trackers, mindfulness apps, and a growing focus on healthy eating are making us all champions of our well-being. So, if you're turning 60 today, your story doesn't end with retirement. It's just the exciting beginning of Act Two, where you can rewrite the script and turn those extra years into a masterpiece of adventure, fulfilment, and maybe even a few encores!

CHAPTER FOUR
Searching for meaning at 60

Are you turning 60? Ditch the dusty rocking chair and dust off your dreams! Yes, the whispers of "you are settled now" may dance around you, however, believe me, 60 is not the curtain call for your life's play. It's the intermission, the threat to grab a sparkling drink, stretch your legs, and rewrite the subsequent act with even bolder strokes.

Remember those issues about growing old? The worry of shrinking horizons, the economic anxieties, the loneliness that may loom like a shadow? They're real, yes, however, they should not steal the display. Let's flip the script. Instead of seeing 60 as the finale, view it as the second act, wherein you shed the costumes of vintage roles and step into the highlight with a newfound purpose.

Forget the outdated perception that at 60, your bucket list is complete. Your existence reports and information are treasures, now not anchors. They're the inspiration on which you can build even grander dreams. Maybe this means sooner or later beginning that pottery studio you constantly craved, volunteering your abilities to help others, or embarking on an adventure as soon as the concept is impossible. It's not approximately what you've already carried out, it's about what ignites your soul now.

Step away from the treadmill of exercises and responsibilities. Let's cross the guilt of prioritizing anyone else. This is a while to polish, to turn the lens inward and ask yourself, "What makes me tick?" What are the passions that shimmer under the surface, ready to be unleashed? Is it painting sunsets, learning a new language, or connecting with vintage pals? Whatever it's far, chase it with the equal enthusiasm you introduced to raising your youngsters or constructing your profession.

And consider, you are no longer on my own on this act. Find your tribe, your fellow renegades who refuse to permit age to dictate their journey. Join a dance magnificence, volunteer at a wildlife centre, or start an ebook club for fellow adventurers. Surround yourself with those who have a good time with your new bankruptcy, and cheer you on as you rewrite the script of your existence.

It's now not about defying age, it is approximately embracing it. Every wrinkle tells a tale, every grey hair a testament to lifestyles well-lived. But your story is not over. So, take a deep breath, improve your glass (of kombucha, in case you wish!), and toast to the interesting opportunities that lie in advance. At 60, the curtain rises at the most thrilling act of all – the only where you write your masterpiece. Go forth, paint your canvas with colourful stories, and display the sector that 60 is simply the beginning, not the give up!

Imagine lifestyles as a meandering river, no longer a stagnant pond. It flows and churns, carving new paths via meadows and mountains, its purpose continuously reshaping with the terrain. Just like that river, our experience of cause isn't some fixed big name you stare upon from afar, it's an ever-evolving dance with the reviews that colour our days.

By achieving 60, that river has carved pretty a journey. We've constructed dams of career and circle of relatives, navigated rapids of loss and pleasure, and sometimes, even discovered ourselves adrift in the shallows of uncertainty. It's no surprise then, that our life which means, that compass of the soul, would possibly want a recalibration.

The years around 60 are a captivating confluence. Loved ones may pass on, careers wind down, and possessions, as soon as so important, appear to lose their lustre. It's just like the river accomplishing an extensive, open plain, uncertain of where to carve its subsequent direction. But inside this uncertainty lies a potent possibility – the hazard to redefine our purpose, to paint a brand new map for our remaining adventure.

Our desires might shift from raising youngsters to nurturing friendships, from chasing promotions to chasing sunsets. The desire to live longer, healthier lives takes root, intertwined with the yearning for connection and means. Each of those desires, these quests, is a critical spark – a flicker of cause waiting to be fanned into a roaring flame.

So, finding a motive at 60 is not approximately stumbling upon a few hidden treasures, it is about actively tending the embers inside. It's approximately listening to the whispers of our hearts, the quiet dreams that linger under the noise of routine. It's approximately stepping off the acquainted route and letting the river carve a new direction, one fueled by interest, ardour, and the deep-seated know-how that our adventure, some distance from ending, is simply beginning its maximum colourful chapter.

So go beforehand, explore the tributaries of your desires, and paddle into the unknown with a coronary heart complete of wish. Remember, 60 isn't the stop of the tale, it's the exciting flip of the web page where you grow to be the author of your grand finale. The river of your lifestyle still has a ways to go, and its cause, like a compass continuously recalibrating, will guide you toward the most magnificent, surprising shores. Let's set sail, not with trepidation, but with the exhilarating information that the most profound discoveries often lie on the other side of uncertainty.

Sixty. The quantity hangs in the air, not but a burden, but a whisper of what can be. Some might see it as the sunset of lifestyles, a time to settle into nicely worn routines and watch the times ebb away like grains of sand. But for others, it's a vibrant sunrise, a risk to crack open lifestyles's treasure chest and declare the untold riches within.

Think of it as a crossroads, not a finishing. You've poured your heart into raising children, constructing careers, and navigating the whirlwind of obligations. Now, the whirlwind calms, presenting an area to breathe, to re-study the map of your coronary heart.

Some, weary warriors at heart, choose to put down their swords. They deserve respite, a danger to savour the easy joys – grandchildren's laughter, the warm temperature of solar-kissed skin, the quiet thrill of an excellent book. For them, 60 is a victory lap, a slow waltz with contentment, in which lifestyles unfold like a gently simmering pot of tea.

But within others, embers nevertheless glow. Dreams tucked away in dusty corners whisper promises of what may be. Maybe it is a formative year ardour for portray that bursts back to existence in colourful watercolour landscapes. Maybe it is a longing for adventure that finds its wings in a solo trek across the Himalayas. Or possibly it's the quiet satisfaction of mentoring young minds, passing at the wisdom gleaned from years of laughter and tears.

The beauty of 60 lies in the freedom of choice. It's a time to shed the masks and expectations worn for many years, to reclaim the soul that danced to a more youthful heart's rhythm. It's a risk to say goodbye to "must haves" and embody "maybe," to paint your masterpiece on the canvas of your closing years.

Some may additionally scoff, whispering of misplaced adolescents and slowing gears. But to folks that concentrate, 60 is the thrilling hum of an engine revving, equipped to propel you into the next chapter. Your enjoyment is a tapestry woven with the threads of lifestyles, a treasure trove of wisdom and resilience. You have something particular to provide, a voice to be heard, a hand to increase.

So, my buddy, step across the brink of 60 with eyes wide open and a coronary heart ablaze. The international stretches before you, a playground painted with possibility. Unfurl your dreams, like sails catching the wind, and let them manual you on an uncharted route. Forget the script existence handed you; write your grand finale, one filled with laughter, pleasure, and the echoes of an existence well-lived. Sixty is not the give up, it's the exhilarating beginning of something extremely good. So, move forth, paint your global in vibrant colours, and display the world that sixty is simply the beginning of something superb.

Stepping into your 60s can feel like standing on the precipice of a full-size, uncharted landscape. The acquainted paths of your younger years fade into the gap, changed using a horizon brimming with each possibility and uncertainty. It's herbal to sense a pang of apprehension, a hesitation before taking the first step into this new terrain.

But right here's the thing: the map may be unknown, but the compass inside you continues to factors authentic north. The fireplace of your spirit, the spark of your interest, the indomitable will that has carried you this some distance – these continue to be undimmed using the passage of time. Ageing may etch lines in your face and silver your hair, but it doesn't touch the essence of who you are.

Think of it like this: you've climbed a mountain, reached the summit, and now stand gazing at a whole new range stretching out earlier than you. The peaks can be different, the challenges specific, however the capabilities you honed on the primary climb – resilience, dedication, adaptability – are still your maximum precious equipment.

So, take a deep breath and let cross of the fear. This uncharted territory is not something to be dreaded however embraced. It's a hazard to shed the skins you have outgrown, to rediscover passions long dormant, to rewrite your narrative in ambitious, unexpected strokes.

Maybe it's getting to know a brand new language, the melody of overseas phrases dancing to your tongue. Maybe it is selecting a paintbrush, transforming blank canvases into vibrant expressions of your soul. Maybe it is volunteering your time and know-how, weaving your existence's tapestry into the material of your community.

The opportunities are as limitless as the stars on a moonless night. Don't permit the fear of the unknown to keep your lower back. Embrace the change, step into the uncharted, and allow your 60s to be the most vibrant, pleasurable bankruptcy of your existence yet. Remember, age is just various, and the best restriction is the one you set for yourself. So, cross forth, expensive adventurer, and paint your masterpiece on the canvas of your last years. The global awaits your next bankruptcy, keen to be dazzled with the aid of the brilliance of your spirit.

CHAPTER FIVE
Life Changes

Defining your Priorities

Think of existence as a grand educated adventure. When we're young, we hurtle through stations at breakneck speed, eyes glued to the windows, eager to see what attractions and stories lie ahead. Every whistle blow pronounces a new journey, and every forestall is a threat to grab a souvenir or embark on a detour. Work is the engine, chugging gradually, pulling us toward the ever-moving horizon of "the weekend," "a new promotion," or that elusive "subsequent degree."

But because the miles tick with the aid of, our priorities subtly shift. The frantic chase for the next thrill gives way to a longing for deeper connections, for stories savoured instead of skimmed. The train slows, pulling into stations for longer stays – possibly to spend afternoons picnicking with children in solar-dappled parks, or to lose ourselves in whispered conversations with loved ones. The rhythm of lifestyles changes, and the beat is no longer dictated via closing dates and conferences however by way of laughter lines etched around eyes and silver threads woven into hair.

And then, somewhere across the bend, we attain the station marked "60." Here, the world seems exclusive from the platform. The engine's roar softens, changed by using the gentle clickety-clack of slower tracks. The whistle's urgent cry changes to a cheerful sigh, announcing the arrival of a unique kind of journey.

For a lot of us, 60 is a time to exchange inflexible schedules and disturbing jobs for the freedom of flexible hours and sun-drenched days. The anxieties of hiking the company ladder are replaced by way of the thrill of tending a flourishing lawn or learning a brand-new craft. Health, as soon as a far-off problem, takes centre level, prompting walks in serene parks and mindful respiratory exercises. Children, those whirlwinds of our younger years, have frequently flown the nest, leaving at the back of precious nests of their personal. The mortgage, as soon as a looming mountain, has contracted to a conceivable hill, and the future, while now not a sprint, stretches out like a scenic coastal street, inviting leisurely exploration.

So, at 60, we step off the train of our past, no longer with resignation, but with a feel of liberation. We've earned the right to alternate inside the breakneck tempo for a waltz with contentment, to change the pressure cooker of ambition for the slow simmer of significant pastimes. This slower tempo allows us to cherish the whispers of our hearts, dirt off lengthy-forgotten desires, and paint our ultimate years in vibrant colours of fulfilment. It's now not approximately retirement, it is approximately reinvention, about embracing the exhilarating possibility of a new bankruptcy, one wherein reports spread like pages in a valuable book, savoured one after the other, with a heart full of gratitude and a spirit aglow with the wisdom of a life properly-lived.

So, dear fellow visitor, step onto the platform of your 60s with a grin. The education might also have slowed, but the adventure has simply ended up even greater enchanting. Breathe inside the fresh air of possibility, sense the solar heat on your skin, and allow the gentle rhythm of your tempo manual to you toward the most gratifying adventure of all: the colourful exploration of a life well-lived, at your candy speed.

Turning 60 isn't only an alternate within the calendar; it is a seismic shift within the landscape of your existence. It's a mountain top you crest, gazing down on the valleys of your past and out in the direction of the uncharted barren region ahead. Exhilarating? Absolutely. Daunting? You guess.

The truth is, reinventing yourself in your 60s is a tango with each opportunity and impediment. The dance floor is great, shimmering with possibilities: passions rekindled, goals revisited, adventures untrodden. But lurking in the shadows are emotional and financial hurdles, ready to trip you up if you're now not prepared.

So, how do you navigate this exhilarating but elaborate terrain? Here's the key: be a strategist, not a gambler. Acknowledge the hurdles, no longer with worry, but with a steely solution. Embrace the emotional challenges, no longer as roadblocks, but as stepping stones to self-discovery. And most importantly, plan your price range with the understanding of a pro-investor, no longer the recklessness of a thrill-seeker.

Emotional hurdles? They are available in diverse forms. Leaving at the back of the acquainted rhythm of your career can be like stepping off a moving teach. The empty nest may echo with a bittersweet silence. And going through health concerns, whether or not yours or those of cherished ones, can be a sobering fact check.

But right here's the turn side: those challenges also can be catalysts for profound boom. Leaving your job can open doorways to long-forgotten passions. The solitude of an empty nest can be the appropriate backdrop for introspection and rediscovering yourself. Dealing with health issues may be a warning call to prioritize well-being and cherish every valuable moment.

The economic hurdle? It's actual, and it desires to be addressed head-on. Retirement savings, investments, and healthcare fees – those aren't glamorous subjects, however, they're the bedrock of your newfound freedom. Planning, budgeting, and in search for professional recommendations are vital steps to make certain your destiny is as brilliant as your desires.

Remember, reinventing yourself in your 60s isn't a solo sprint; it is a collaborative marathon. Lean on your family for assistance, steering, and the occasional truth take a look at. Seek out groups of like-minded people who are also waltzing with exchange. And, most importantly, spend money on yourself –studying new talents, exploring hidden abilities, and nurturing your emotional well-being.

So, dear buddy, step onto the dance floor of your 60s with eyes wide open and a heart complete of hope. Acknowledge the hurdles, but don't allow them to define your adventure. Embrace the emotionally demanding situations as possibilities for increase, and plan your finances with the shrewdness of a seasoned explorer. Remember, the greatest adventures regularly lie beyond the familiar, and the most top-notch landscapes are often discovered at the course much less travelled. So, take that first step, maintain your head high, and permit your 60s to be the most magnificent, surprising, and gratifying chapter of your existence.

Understanding Psychological Changes in Old Age

Sixty!!!! It's not simply several etched on a birthday cake; it's a threshold, a doorway to a grand, uncharted chapter within the e-book of your life. But like all exact stories, this new bankruptcy has its twists and turns, its hidden anxieties and shadows lurking at the edges. Stepping into your 60s can be exhilarating, sure, but it could additionally be a psychological tightrope stroll, worrying a delicate stability among the fun of the unknown and the fear of falling.

The maximum apparent hurdle, the elephant inside the room with a smartly packed suitcase, is the void left by retirement. For years, your days have been constructed across the constant rhythm of labour, a shape that all at once crumbles away, leaving you with... what? An aching emptiness, a gnawing worry of purposelessness? It's ordinary. Imagine a seasoned dancer abruptly stripped of the degree, the spotlight, and the familiar choreography. Disorientation is inevitable.

But underneath the floor, more subtle shadows dance. There's the quiet sadness that includes witnessing the passage of time, the empty chairs at own family gatherings, and the recollections that sparkle like fireflies in the twilight. And there may be the tension, the gnawing uncertainty approximately destiny: "What if my savings aren't sufficient?" "What if I emerge as isolated?" "What if that is it?"

But wait, earlier than you fall into the abyss of existential dread, take a deep breath and don't forget this: these challenges, even though real, aren't insurmountable. They can be the very gasoline that propels you into the most pleasing years of your life.

The worry of vacancy? It may be a catalyst for rediscovering long-forgotten passions, embarking on innovative trips, or reconnecting with a circle of relatives and community in ways you never idea viable. The anxieties about destiny? They can be a wake-up call, prompting you to devise, to adapt, to build a new experience of safety and cause.

Remember, your 60s aren't a finishing, but a remarkable reimagining. Embrace the mentally demanding situations as opportunities for growth, self-discovery, for reinventing yourself on a canvas splashed with colourful colorings of revel in and understanding. Lean on loved ones, construct new assist networks, and try to find expert help if wished – you are not by yourself on this dance at the tightrope.

So, my friend, step into your 60s with courage, now not trepidation. Let the anxieties be whispers, not roars. The shadows are there, yes, however so is the radiant sunlight, ready to bathe your direction in warmth and opportunity. This new chapter is yours to write, and its mental complexities aren't roadblocks, but brushstrokes, ready to colour the most magnificent masterpiece of your life yet.

Life after 60 can be a colourful tapestry woven with new adventures and rediscovered joys. But like any rich tapestry, there might be a few knots and snags here and there. It's essential to be aware of some common mental bumps that could appear along the way, now not to scare you off, but to help you navigate them with grace and resilience.

Remember, no longer does anybody review all of those, and even if you stumble upon one, it does not mean it has to outline your adventure. Think of it like encountering a detour on a road trip – you're taking a unique path, discovering new points of interest, and still reaching your destination, perhaps despite a richer tale to tell.

One common feeling is the experience of vacancy that may come with retirement. Years of shape and purpose vanish, leaving you wondering, "Now what?" But this can additionally be a fertile ground for growth. Think of it as a blank canvas, ready to be splashed with the colours of newfound passions, rekindled creativity, and deeper connections with cherished ones.

Then there is the quiet ache of disappointment. Time marches on, and with it, cherished memories may turn out to be bittersweet and loved ones are probably misplaced. It's ok to renowned this disappointment, permit it to wash over you, and then, like a spring flower pushing through the soil, allow yourself to bloom once more. Find solace in memories, cherish the prevailing moments, and build new connections that bring warmth and laughter.

And allow us no longer to forget the occasional tension that whispers "What if?" What in case your savings are not sufficient? What in case you end up remoted? These issues are herbal, however, do not let them paralyze you. Take control, plan for destiny, and attain for guide. Remember, you are now not alone in this journey, and there are numerous palms prepared that will help you navigate the uncertainties.

The key is to embrace these psychological bumps as a part of the human experience, now not roadblocks to happiness. They can be catalysts for self-discovery, resilience, and a deeper appreciation for the prevailing moment. So, step into your 60s with eyes wide open and a coronary heart complete of wish. Remember, each knot and snag provides a unique texture to your tapestry, making it even more beautiful and rich. Enjoy the detours, relish the quiet moments, and paint your masterpiece of satisfying lifestyles.

We will talk about some prevalent psychological conditions to be aware of, while not everyone experiences all of them or even the majority of them:

Old age Anxiety

Life, just like a flowing river, is rarely stagnant. While a few modifications ripple lightly, others crash like rapids, forcing us to navigate uncharted waters. Stepping into your 60s maybe this kind of cutting-edge, churning familiar workouts and tossing up unexpected demanding situations. One mainly elaborate eddy – an underestimation, is not it? – is that even high-quality adjustments can stir up a tidal wave of hysteria.

It's counterintuitive, we recognize. We dream of retirement, fantasize about escaping the cubicle cage, and yearn for a journey. But when the day arrives, the fact can be surprisingly unsettling. Decades of building a lifestyle around the constant thrum of habitual vanish, changed by using an unnerving vacuum. The clock, once a dictator, becomes a silent judge, and the query "What now?" echoes inside the hollow spaces of our days.

This, my friend, isn't some weird private failing; it is a dance with human nature. We are creatures of dependency, comforted via the predictable pulse of the ordinary. Our days, like clockwork, offer a comforting melody of work, our own family, and familiar rituals. Stepping off that properly-worn course, even when it's to chase rainbows, can trigger a surge of anxiety.

Imagine, if you will, a seasoned sailor all of sudden swapping his charts for a hot air balloon. Exhilarating? Undoubtedly. But additionally nerve-wracking. The wind whispers of uncharted skies, the floor shrinks under you, and the familiar compass of habitual spins uselessly.

But keep on, before you allow the anxiety to drag you beneath, remember this: the vastness you fear is also a canvas of opportunity. Retirement is not just about ditching the alarm clock; it is approximately reclaiming your canvas and painting it with colourful colours of rediscovered goals, rekindled passions, and a renewed reference to cherished ones.

The anxieties are actual, yes, however, they are no longer monsters; they're shadows dancing at the wall. Acknowledge them, understand them, and then, like a captain gaining knowledge to navigate through the celebs, discover your new constellation of causes. Lean on your family, construct new assist networks, and take into account, that there's an entire fleet of fellow adventurers obtainable, cruising uncharted waters with you.

So, my pal, include the cutting-edge alternate, even though it throws you a little off stability. Let the anxieties be whispers, not roars. The open waters you fear keep untold treasures, and the journey, with all its eddies and currents, is yours to chart. Take a deep breath, unfurl your sails, and set your direction to an adventure-crammed, tension-tamed sundown of your lifestyles. You've got this, captain!

Strategies to Defeat Anxiety at 60

Life after 60 can sense like a blank canvas, the old paint dried and cracked. Routine, that once comforting hum, fades into echo. The void it leaves may be daunting, the query "What now?" echoing inside the silence. But worry no longer, my buddy, for this empty canvas, is also an invite to create, to colour a masterpiece of existence unlike any earlier.

The key to filling this canvas lies in finding new hues, and new brushstrokes. Hobbies, the ones neglected pals of our more youthful years, beckon us back into their warm embrace. They provide shape, no longer inside the inflexible grip of habitual, but inside the rhythm of discovery, the pleasure of learning, and the mild nudge of motive.

Think of it like this: the acquainted route you walked for years has reached a fork. One route ends in the quiet solitude of endless days, the opposite, a winding trail dotted with vibrant opportunities. Gardening beckons with the earthy scent of freshly baked soil and the quiet pleasure of nurturing existence. Golf gives the camaraderie of the clubhouse, the joys of a properly positioned shot, and the sparkling air that whispers secrets in the rustle of leaves. Tennis paints the sky with the arc of a great serve, the laughter of your partner echoing in the crisp air. And Charity paintings, like a broom, dipped in kindness, allow you to paint the world in brighter hues, leaving a legacy far past your canvas.

But recollect, the most vibrant hues come from a balanced palette. Choose interests that mix bodily interest with the warmth of social interaction. The sweat of exertion washes away fear, whilst the laughter of shared moments chases away isolation. Join a gardening club, a friendly foursome on the golfing course, a doubles fit packed with laughter or discover a charity that ignites your passion. In these shared spaces, you may not most effectively reclaim a sense of routine but find new connections, new friendships, and new threads woven into the tapestry of your lifestyles.

So, embrace the blank canvas, my friend. Don't permit the anxiety of vacancy to preserve you again. Pick up a brand new brush, dip it in the colourful colours of possibility, and begin painting. Step onto the winding trail of hobbies, allow the solar heat your skin and breathe in the clean air of lifestyles reborn. Remember, with each stroke, every colour, you are not simply filling a canvas, you are creating a masterpiece – a vibrant, fulfilling bankruptcy of your life, painted in the golden shades of your 60s.

Depression that comes with age

The range sixty hangs inside the air, a whisper of change, a promise of uncharted paths. For a few, it is a jubilant melody, a drumbeat of freedom subsequently arrived. But for others, it can be a disquieting harmony, a tango with shadows lurking inside the corners of their hearts. Depression, that unwelcome guest, can tap at the shoulder even of the most spirited souls in the face of this type of seismic shift.

Retirement, a long-dreamed-of break out from the daily grind, can all of sudden feel like a considerable, empty playground without swings or sandcastles. Jobs, as soon as anchors of cause, leave vacant spaces in our days, the phantom time limits still ticking in our minds. Even ventures into new territories, like beginning a business, maybe exhilarating one second and terrifying the following, the fun of opportunity jostling with the gnawing fear of the unknown.

The irony stings – all this excess strength, the type that once fueled ambitious climbs and tight cut-off dates, now spills over in anxious twitches and stressed nights. Or worse, it becomes a heavyweight, draining the very will to get off the bed. We swing like pendulums among frenetic highs and paralyzing lows, the emotional tide washing us ashore on unexpected beaches of uncertainty.

But take into account, my buddy, even the solar cast shadows. These bouts of darkness, while unsettling, are not aberrations; they may be threads woven into the tapestry of human enjoyment. Everyone, at some unspecified time in the future, confronts the whispers of tension and the pain of sadness. It's how we manage them, how we dance with those shadows, that determines the rhythm of our lives.

If the darkness lingers, and will become a deafening roar rather than a murmur, know that you aren't on my own. Seek help, discover your mild. Talk to loved ones, construct an assisted community, and reach out to specialists who let you navigate these emotional shoals. Remember, electricity does not lie in denying the shadows, but in dancing with them, in locating the glints of desire that pierce through the gloom.

So, take a deep breath, pricey friend. Embrace the complexities of this new bankruptcy. Let the anxiety be a whisper, not a scream. The course in advance may be untrodden, however you aren't on my own. Find your pursuits, your passions, your connections – they're the lighthouses as a way to manual you via the storms. And above all, don't forget, that even the darkest night subsequently offers way to dawn. Your 60s might also hold shadows, but in addition, they maintain the solar, ready to bathe your adventure in warm temperatures and possibility. So, step into the mild, my pal, and paint your radiant masterpiece on the canvas of your life.

Try as much as possible to seek professional help when you feel some abnormal symptoms in your body when you are advanced in age. Below are some emotions or abnormal feelings you need to check:

➤ Intense melancholy, emptiness, or hopelessness that seem to surround you.

➤ Anger outbursts, impatience, or frustration, especially about trivial or ordinarily unimportant issues.

➤ Loss of enjoyment or interest in formerly pleasurable activities, such as sports, hobbies, or sex.

➢ Disruptions in sleep, such as hypersomnia or insomnia (sleeping too much).

➢ General exhaustion or malaise, making even little chores feel laborious.

➢ Unusual dietary changes, quick weight loss or increase.

➢ Sluggish or delayed speech, movement, or thought habits.

➢ Consistent emotions of remorse or worthlessness, focusing on mistakes or self-blame in the past.

➢ Problems with memory, concentration, decision-making, and thought (more than normal).

➢ Thoughts of suicide, death, or previous suicide attempts.

Take your Financial Life Seriously

Turning 60 is like crossing a threshold into a sun-dappled orchard of possibilities. But in contrast to the ripe fruit hanging within reach, a number of those possibilities – like retirement, career changes, or entrepreneurial ventures – come wrapped in a layer of monetary concerns, ripe for careful peeling. It's no longer about raining to your parade, my pal, but about ensuring your dance with change has a cushy floor under your toes.

The fact is, your dating with money may want a bit of recalibrating as you cross this threshold. Retirement, that lengthy-awaited getaway from the cubicle cage, frequently comes with a mild however organisational adjustment to income. Changing careers would possibly offer a clean start, but the monetary direction might be bumpier at the beginning. And even that exciting dream of launching your commercial enterprise is a thrilling curler coaster, with financial dips and climbs as interesting as the thrills.

This does not suggest your goals are out of reach, in no way. It sincerely means a little coaching can turn them from mirages into oases. Predicting what your new earnings may look like is prime. Dust off your retirement plans, crunch a few numbers, and be sincere with yourself – can your modern lifestyle climate cause a decrease in earnings? If now not, are you able to regulate? Perhaps downsizing, revisiting spending conduct, or even picking up some brief work can smooth the transition.

For career adjustments and entrepreneurial ventures, the monetary roadmap is probably less simple. Research salaries in your new discipline, and element in any extra schooling costs, and be realistic about approximately the time it'd take to attain monetary stability. As in your commercial enterprise dream, create a comprehensive marketing strategy, search for expert advice, and prepare for a length of bootstrapping earlier than the earnings start rolling in.

Remember, practice isn't approximately shackling yourself to spreadsheets; it is approximately giving your dreams wings. Knowing your economic landscape allows you to take calculated dangers, and to chase those juicy, solar-dappled possibilities with self-assurance. It's about making informed decisions so your 60s become a symphony of fulfilment, now not a discordant concerto of economic worries.

So, earlier than you dive headfirst into that entrepreneurial bounce of religion, or step into retirement's solar-soaking wet meadows, take a moment to map your economic journey. Talk to advisors, crunch a few numbers, and make a plan that aligns with your goals and your bank account. Remember, my pal, economic attention isn't always a buzzkill; it is the magic compass that guarantees your 60s are filled not just with opportunities, but with the freedom to include all of them. So, cross forth, chart your direction, and paint your masterpiece on the canvas of your financially steady future. The sun-dappled orchard awaits!

Turning 60 is not pretty much cake and candles; it's approximately stepping onto a brand new degree to your lifestyle's play, a stage bathed in both the golden glow of opportunity and the gentle spotlight of mirrored image. But much like any excellent play, a fulfilling act two relies upon clearing the clutter from act one. And in that clutter, hidden among the memories and milestones, are regularly the cobwebs of debt.

Now, debt is not a monster below the bed, waiting to gobble up your retirement goals. It's a fact for lots, woven into the fabric of existence. But at 60, it's time to take into account its weight, now not just to your shoulders, but on the shoulders of those you love. Leaving at the back of a legacy of unpaid bills isn't a burden you need to bypass on your youngsters and grandchildren. It's now not a measure of their worth, but a reminder of your unfinished commercial enterprise.

So, let's talk approximately credit playing cards, those plastic temptations that whisper with guarantees of immediate gratification however often go away at the back of a sour aftertaste of high interest and wasted budget. Think of them like emotional leeches, sucking the joy out of each purchase. Now is the time to break free from their grip, reclaim your financial independence, and paint your 60s with the vibrant colours of a debt-loose canvas.

But do not be crushed by the mountain of bills; take it step by step, card through card. Start with the one that is been feasting for your pockets with the very best hobby charge, that monetary bloodsucker stealing the sunshine out of your future. Tackle it with laser recognition, a warrior wielding a budget as your sword. Once it is slain, move on to the subsequent, chipping away at the debt like a sculptor revealing a masterpiece within.

And then, there is the loan, the anchor that tethers us to the shorelines of financial duty. While owning a domestic is a blessing, the month-to-month payment can sense like a constant tug on the tide, pulling you far from the open waters of freedom. But imagine, just believe, entering your 60s with that anchor lifted, changed by way of the gentle breeze of a paid-off residence. The weight on your shoulders eases, changed via the exhilarating lightness of proudly owning your haven, debt-loose and serene.

Remember, clearing your financial decks is not pretty much numbers; it is approximately peace of mind, approximately giving yourself the present of serenity to your golden years. It's about leaving a legacy of no longer just memories, but financial freedom, a gift that resonates ways beyond the material and whispers "I love you" in every breath of economic security.

So, expensive buddy, snatch your finances as your guard, your economic plan as your map, and embark on this adventure of debt-slaying. It might not be smooth, there may be moments of doubt and fatigue, however, the reward – a destiny bathed in the sunshine of financial freedom – is worth every ounce of effort. Take it one step at a time, one card at a time, one mortgage payment at a time, and paint your 60s with the colourful colours of a debt-free masterpiece, a legacy of affection and knowledge for generations to come back. You've been given this, adventurer!

CHAPTER SIX
Actions to Take at 60

❖ *Create your "me" time*

Life at 60 is like cracking open a book you have loved for years, however this time, you in the end have the luxury to savour every chapter at your very own tempo. The youngsters, once whirlwind tornadoes stressful regular attention, have blossomed into grounded people, spinning their own stories in the global. This, my pal, is the exhale after a lifetime of inhaling, the gap to finally whisper "me" and watch it bloom into a colourful "mine."

For Wyman, a woman who delved deeper into the sector of ageing with postgraduate work in gerontology, this "me" time is a symphony of rediscovery. The anxieties that once hummed like a consistent bassline in her days – homework closing dates, scraped knees, career choices – have softened into a gentle melody. In their area, a new rhythm emerges, one where self-care isn't a guilty indulgence, but a critical harmony on the grand rating of existence.

This isn't to mention the maternal melody fades away; it transforms. The fear lines etched through sleepless nights morph into threads of satisfaction, woven into the tapestry of her kid's successes. Phone calls are not full of frantic updates but with laughter-laced testimonies of their adventures. And the ever-present "mom" badge, worn with unwavering willpower, is now gently slipped on and off, permitting area for another badge to polish – the colourful "me" badge, proudly proclaiming a newfound chapter of exploration and personal increase.

It's not selfishness, this "me" time; it is self-preservation, the nourishing of a well that has given so freely for so long. It's picking up a dusty paintbrush and discovering hues you in no way knew you held, hues that splash onto the canvas of your life with an exhilarating vibrancy. It's taking that once-forgotten dance magnificence, letting your body sway to the rhythm of its joy. It's indulging in a solo trip, the wind whispering secrets and techniques for your ear as you explore unknown streets, savouring the solitude.

Remember, "me" is not the enemy of "mom" or "grandmother"; it is their accomplice, their cheerleader, their associate in this dance called lifestyles. So, my buddy, as you switch 60, include the "me" that whispers inside. Make time for quiet contemplation, adventurous tours, for moments of natural, unadulterated indulgence. Let your "me" bloom alongside your cherished roles, enriching them with newfound vibrancy and reminding you that your tale, your adventure of self-discovery, is still being written, waiting to be painted inside the golden colours of your 60s.

Take these few actions:

- Give your inner child the reins for a while. Go play!
- Remember, self-care isn't selfish; it's mandatory for awesome humans like you.
- Treat yourself like the VIP you are. You deserve it!
- Let your "me" time be your secret weapon for staying young and fabulous.

❖ *A letter to loved ones*

We're now not speaking about a sentimental letter here. We're talking about a letter in your circle of relatives that lists all of your medical doctors, legal professionals, and monetary planners, as well as the locations of your secure deposit container, wills, banks, and investment assets.

How is this a letter of affection? It can greatly reduce confusion and struggle whilst you skip away, says Mark Brown, co-proprietor of Brown & Tedstrom Wealth Management in Denver, "so it is one of the most realistic and loving things you can do to your family." (Actually, it's a very good list for everybody who's ageing to have as a personal directory of important information)

These letters could serve your family and friends for a long time to remember your life.

A Compass of Care:

Instead of a laundry list of doctors and attorneys, consider crafting a heartfelt letter that serves as a compass for your loved ones when you're long gone. This compass would not point north however towards the experts who apprehend you best and the places wherein your wishes are laid naked. It's now not pretty much logistics, however approximately leaving a legacy of readability and ease, whispered within the language of love and practicality.

A Map of Memories and Matters:

Think of this letter as a treasure map, now not for buried gold, but for the things that count – your clinical records, your financial knowledge, and the connections you've constructed throughout your lifestyles. It's about gifting your own family the ability to navigate the once-in-a-while chilly waters of loss with a warmth born of your foresight and affection.

A Bridge Across Time:

This letter is not a goodbye, but a bridge out of your life to theirs. It's dangerous to increase your love beyond your final breath, offering solace in the shape of know-how and guidance. Imagine the comfort your own family will discover in knowing you have not just left them with memories, but also with a clear pathway through the practicalities that comply with your passing.

A Whisper of Foresight:

This letter isn't always about cold facts and passwords; it's approximately a whispered promise of peace of thought. It's approximately announcing, "Even though I'm not here bodily, I've carried out the entirety I can to ensure your journey is easy, and your direction illuminated." It's a testimony to a love that transcends time, presenting now not simply emotional aid, but additionally, the sensible gear to navigate hard terrain.

A Gift of Clarity:

Think of this letter as a final act of selflessness, a gift of readability wrapped inside the gentle tissue of love. It's about sparing your circle of relatives the fog of bewilderment and grief by handing them a torch, letting them navigate the uncertainties with a lightness born of your forethought. It's no longer approximately possessions, but approximately the peace that comes from understanding you've made their passage a bit easier.

This can serve as an example of a letter. Read and draft your letters today.

My dearest family,

Life, as they say, is a grand and unpredictable journey. While we all hope for sunny skies and smooth roads, the occasional detour or downpour is inevitable. And while none of us wish to contemplate the end of the path, preparing for it – not out of fear, but out of love – is perhaps the most practical, and yes, loving, thing we can do for those we hold dear.

So, in that spirit of love and practicality, I'm writing this letter not with sentimental prose, but with a clear head and a full heart. It's a letter filled with details, addresses, and passwords – an essential map to navigate the sometimes-murky waters of life after my time.

Think of it as a treasure chest, not of gold and jewels, but of information – a legacy built not of riches, but of clarity and ease. Within these pages, you'll find the coordinates of the doctors who know me best, the lawyers who understand my affairs, and the financial guides who have charted my financial course. You'll discover the hidden keys to my safe deposit box, the location of my will, and the compass pointing to my bank accounts and investments.

It may seem impersonal, this litany of numbers and names. But trust me, my love, it's born from the deepest affection. Imagine the burden lifted from your shoulders if, in a moment of grief and uncertainty, you didn't have to grapple with the unknowns, the frantic searches, the frustrating dead ends. Imagine if, instead, you had a clear path, a roadmap built with love, leading you through the necessary steps with a minimum of confusion and heartache.

This, my dears, is my gift to you – not a teary farewell, but a practical hug, a whispered assurance that even in my absence, I've done everything I can to make your journey a little smoother, a little less filled with bewilderment. It's not about clinging to possessions; it's about letting go with grace, knowing that your inheritance is not just material, but also the peace of mind that comes from a clear path forward.

So, keep this letter safe, my loves. Treat it as a cherished guide, a testament to the unwavering love that binds us, even across the veil of time. And remember, while it may seem like a cold exchange of facts, know that every address, every password, is etched with the warmth of my affection, whispering "I love you" in a language of clarity and care.

With all my love,

Your forever-present, even-in-absence,
always-loving (Napoleon)

❖ *Reduce your spending, save and invest*

Stepping into your 60s can sense like final chapter and peek on the clean page of the subsequent. It's a time for fresh beginnings, regularly accompanied by a change of surroundings – like Patricia Vacca, who traded her circle of relatives home for a vibrant retirement network in Silver Springs, Maryland. But what about all the ones collected assets? They hold reminiscences, certain, but additionally, they whisper stories of unused areas and capability muddle on your new, smaller haven.

Patricia failed to just field the whole thing up and hire a dusty garage unit (a graveyard for forgotten treasures and a drain for your wallet). No, she embraced a better, savvier approach: a little online magic referred to as MaxSold.Com.

Think of it as a virtual backyard sale on steroids. MaxSold would not simply list your dusty lamps and chipped teacups; they take lovely snapshots, write enticing descriptions, and deal with the entire public sale process from beginning to completion. All Patricia had to do became a factor and say "Sell!" Then, like a fairy godmother with a knack for online marketing, MaxSold whisked in, transformed her "treasures" into virtual gold, and introduced a cool $1,000 directly into her pocket – all within per week!

And Patricia is a long way from on my own. Barry Gordon, MaxSold's CEO, is famous for a mystery many neglects: "You don't need a mansion complete with antiques to thrive in an auction." Their usual customer is a person such as you, a savvy soul for your 60s, equipped to shed possessions and embody a lighter, brighter future. MaxSold has visible clients stroll away with earnings ranging from $three,000 to a jaw-dropping $10,000 – all from gadgets they might have tossed into a garage sale or worse, a landfill.

Of course, MaxSold does not work its magic-free. They take a 30% reduction of the public sale winnings, an honest alternative for the strain-loose, finger-lifting-loose experience they offer. And if MaxSold isn't in your town yet, worry not! Many online systems offer comparable services, allowing you to become your auctioneer, connecting with a wider pool of capacity consumers, and transforming your downsizing adventure from a chore into a treasure hunt for both you and your keen clients.

So, expensive buddy, as you turn the web page on your next bankruptcy, bear in mind, that less can be extra, and letting go would not mean saying goodbye. Embrace the possibilities of online auctions, turn your unused treasures into golden nuggets, and paint your new, downsized lifestyles with the vibrant colourations of economic freedom and a lighter, litter-unfastened soul. The magic awaits, only a click away!

❖ *Insure your life*

When people reach their 60s, it's common for them to remember letting them pass off their existing coverage policies, mainly if they have widespread assets to cover any final economic responsibilities. While having enough finances is sincerely a high-quality state of affairs, monetary guide Mark Brown shows taking a more in-depth appearance before you make a decision.

One component to bear in mind is if you still have an amazing mortgage. According to the Consumer Financial Protection Bureau, many older people are getting into retirement with more mortgage debt than preceding generations. Keeping your existing insurance coverage in such cases ought to offer protection internet to your own family in the event of your passing.

Additionally, when you have other debts or monetary liabilities that could probably jeopardize your own family's monetary safety after your demise, it can be well worth keeping your life insurance insurance. Mark Brown emphasizes the significance of comparing your specific monetary state of affairs and the ability risks concerned earlier than letting cross off your lifestyle insurance policy.

❖ *Set Goals that scare you and make you come alive*

Embarking on your journey towards the existence you choose begins with planning for destiny.

Take a considerate study of your lifestyles to date and reflect on the studies you would possibly have overlooked. It's a time to keep in mind the things you've constantly desired to do but have not had the threat to explore. By placing realistic and potential goals, you might not overwhelm yourself, yet you will introduce an experience of novelty and excitement into your lifestyles. This technique guarantees that you always have new and pleasurable experiences to look forward to.

❖ *Become an Entrepreneur*

Consider the possibility of venturing into entrepreneurship when you're in your 60s, as around one-0.33 of people in this age organization specifically choose to work independently. It's a length in existence where many have amassed a few financial savings, reached the top in their careers, and often locate themselves with grown-up children who've moved out.

This level offers an opportune second to begin your enterprise, mainly whilst future career development in conventional employment appears less probable. The thought is to preferably launch your venture 3 years earlier than your deliberate retirement. This strategic timing allows for personal development, the enlargement of your expert network, and the introduction of an additional earnings stream—all while still playing the perks of your current activity.

Even if the entrepreneurial journey faces preliminary challenges, fulfilment is still inside reach. Statistics display that older entrepreneurs tend to acquire more fulfilment than their more youthful counterparts. This underscores the resilience, enjoyment, and flexibility that include age, proving that beginning a business later in life can result in significant accomplishments.

It's important not to allow the notion that you're too vintage to maintain you returned from pursuing something new. Many businesspeople started their ventures later in their lifestyles, showcasing that age should not be a barrier to achievement. Icons like Walt Disney, Charles Flint (IBM), Harland "Colonel" Sanders (Kentucky Fried Chicken), Ray Kroc (McDonald's), and numerous others carried out brilliant fulfilment despite launching their organizations later on their journeys.

The most effective person convincing yourself that success is out of reach is you. Remember, it's in no way too past due to embark on the adventure of launching your venture. The testimonies of those successful individuals function as a powerful reminder that age is not a restricting aspect on the subject of realizing your aspirations and creating a meaningful effect.

❖ *Giving to your neighbourhood*

Engaging in a network carrier is a sizeable and impactful step you can take in your lifestyle.

There are numerous ways to make contributions, from volunteering for charitable companies to sharing your know-how with kids or leading workshops. For people under strong pressure, there's even the opportunity to initiate a social movement that addresses a motive close to your coronary heart.

It's important to avoid taking flight into seclusion, as connecting with the network brings a sense of reason and relevance. By actively participating and giving lower back, you not simplest make a fantastic impact on others but also foster a deeper connection to the world around you, enriching your very own existence in the technique.

CONCLUSION

The desire for quieter pursuits and relationships is evident as I grow older. I no longer engage in the endless debates and rivalries that require a fiery spirit. While my family's toughness gives me hope for the future, I cannot ignore the fact that mortality is looming. Losing peers and a sibling in recent times has made me realize that death is inevitable. It is a spiritual challenge that we must all face.

I find it unjust that we are often left grappling with death in our advanced age when our physical and mental faculties have dwindled. The tools we once used to process and prepare for the end are themselves ending. It is almost cruel how nature and time relentlessly siege upon our mortal bodies.

As I still have my wits intact, I know that my work is to face down death proactively before it further encroaches. I must make peace with letting go of this worldly dance while I still have rhythm and mobility. Before the music fades, there is still some living left for me to do. But I hear the clock ticking towards my final bows.

Given the march of time and the inevitability of death, I no longer think that 60 is too early to start preparing for life's final transition. In my younger days, I was passionate about creating radical social change. However, I have come to understand that the world's entrenched brokenness will not change anytime soon.

Even with medical advances, death remains an absolute barrier that no one can escape. At 60, I have come to terms with my impermanence and gained peace by facing it head-on.

While I celebrate improved health and activity levels, I also realize that it is dangerous to avoid wrestling with existential questions that come with ageing. I want to live fully while embracing mortality and not deny it through endless striving for a fountain of youth vitality.

Preparing for all aspects of my life's concluding chapter can unlock meaning and closure in a culture that hides death away. I hope to approach my final years with reverence and wonder at the sacred privilege of inhabiting every moment fully. Making peace with endings opens space for deeper connections and for pouring love into this world, knowing that our time is precious. With grace, I may be able to guide others in their journeys grappling with life's ephemeral nature as well.

Back in 1970, life unfolded like a predictable story. Retirement would fall around 64, giving you a leisurely six-and-a-half years to bask in retirement before the grand finale. But things have changed dramatically. Modern medicine has become a wizard, waving its wand against disease and extending our healthy years beyond our wildest dreams. Smoking, once the ubiquitous villain, has lost its grip, and health awareness has become fashionable. Those turning 60 in 2010 could confidently envision themselves not only working the entire decade but also enjoying a vibrant lifestyle until at least 78.7 years old. That's an additional 14 valuable years compared to our counterparts from 1970 – enough time to write a whole new chapter, filled with adventures, passions, and perhaps even a second career! So, let's embrace the exciting rewrite and ditch the old retirement script. Your 60s are just the beginning of a new act, full of possibilities waiting to be explored.

Addressing mortality

The church has a longstanding tradition of addressing how individuals should navigate life in the face of mortality and pondering the uncertainties of what lies beyond death, spanning two millennia. This emphasis is not arbitrary but is rooted in the wisdom of adopting a "both/and" perspective rather than an "either/or" stance. Pastors who dedicate part of their sermons to topics like "the resurrection of the dead and the life of the world to come" are worthy of commendation rather than criticism.

This focus on the afterlife becomes particularly relevant for some members of the congregation who may be grappling with the profound shift that comes with reaching the age of 60 or even older. Moments of transition, be it a change in employment, the establishment of a business, or retirement, inherently carry a significant amount of stress.

Advancing in age, however, comes with its own set of advantages, and one notable aspect is the wealth of experience gained over the years. This experience provides the foresight to anticipate potential challenges that may arise during major life changes, drawing from the reservoir of prior transformative experiences.

Reaching the age of 60 is not a barrier to transformative life changes; in fact, it can be an empowering time. By conducting thorough research, adequate preparation, and strategic planning, individuals can successfully embark on a journey of transformation, feeling a sense of pride in their achievements. The age of 60, rather than being a limitation, can mark the beginning of a new and fulfilling chapter in one's life.

www.ingramcontent.com/pod-product-compliance
Lightning Source LLC
Chambersburg PA
CBHW071053290526
45795CB00004B/1467